# Radiating Consciousness

My Journey of Growth Through the Science of Mind.

Rev. Michael J. Kearney, DD

**BALBOA.**
PRESS

A DIVISION OF HAY HOUSE

Balboa Press books may be ordered through booksellers or by contacting:

Balboa Press
A Division of Hay House
1663 Liberty Drive
Bloomington, IN 47403
www.balboapress.com
1 (877) 407-4847

Because of the dynamic nature of the Internet, any web addresses or
links contained in this book may have changed since publication and
may no longer be valid. The views expressed in this work are solely those
of the author and do not necessarily reflect the views of the publisher,
and the publisher hereby disclaims any responsibility for them.

The author of this book does not dispense medical advice or prescribe the use
of any technique as a form of treatment for physical, emotional, or medical
problems without the advice of a physician, either directly or indirectly. The
intent of the author is only to offer information of a general nature to help
you in your quest for emotional and spiritual well-being. In the event you use
any of the information in this book for yourself, which is your constitutional
right, the author and the publisher assume no responsibility for your actions.

Any people depicted in stock imagery provided by Getty Images are
models, and such images are being used for illustrative purposes only.
Certain stock imagery © Getty Images.

Print information available on the last page.

ISBN: 978-1-5043-9801-5 (sc)
ISBN: 978-1-5043-9802-2 (e)

Balboa Press rev. date: 03/19/2018

# Contents

*"Radiating Consciousness I am forever investigating into the depths of the soul of who I am."*

This is the purpose statement I wrote for myself in 2008, shortly after my 60th birthday. This was a time for new beginnings in my life. I was reaching into an awareness that though many of my siblings, friends and colleagues were discussing the idea of retirement, I was only reaching the half way point in my earthly life.

Somewhere in my childhood I had considered what the measurement of age was and how would I grow to be older than everybody I knew. It was then that I considered that to live to 120 would be my goal. I don't remember if I considered how I would do this, but the number remained with me. Whenever a question would come up in conversation or some workshop asking me to vision into the future of my life, I recalled living to 120.

The year before my 60th birthday I found myself engaged in several life changing activities. After nearly 25 years of working in the mental health field as a recreation counselor, cottage supervisor and Group Home Administrator, I had earned my Ordination as a Licensed Minister in the United Church of Religious Science. My plans were to travel and basically semi-retire and live out of my motor home. I had survived two long term partners, both died of AIDS related causes. Each of these relationships had provided direction, love and healing awareness to my experience. Knowing that I could not prevent death, I discovered that I found new meaning in life by being with death. I had also thought that I would not be in another long-term relationship at this stage of my life and career. Although

I never gave up the opportunity to use affirmative prayer or ask others to pray for me in regards to relationship. The past twelve years seemed to confirm that I would remain single.

Closing the non-profit organization that contained the group home operation would take some time and effort. I set out to "put my affairs in order" as people often say and used some of this time to travel. Central and South America had a strong calling and I would make several trips including two to travel the Inca trail to Machu Picchu. These trips allowed for a deep spiritual shift to happen within my soul and my affairs. On two of the trips I meet up with a Shaman, neither planned, and both times I experienced a deepening beyond words.

This experience of life transformation can truly rock the boat of life and call upon your inner power to rise to the occasion or perish. It has taken three years to close out the group home organization and all the holdings. At the same time, I was hired full time to be the Senior Minister at the Palm Springs Church of Religious Science. The synchronicity is not lost on my thoughts or left out of my material for Sunday messages. When you make plans, Spirit laughs and reveals what is really meant to happen. Grateful that I am aware of this, I did not resist (too much) and allowed events to flow through my life as God would have it so. The process has graphically demonstrated that there is no denying that consciousness, once set in motion, will lavish upon every individual the abundance and the enthusiasm to which they are open to receive.

My experience and efforts spent in the group home operation had allowed for the development of leadership skills, strengths and some cash reserves. When I was offered the position of Senior Minister in 2006, they had recently lost their minister to a fatal disease and their bank account cash to embezzlement. Suffice it to say, "The ship was adrift without a skipper and there was no gold in the treasure chest." Could I accept the position, guide the members through grief, loss and healing and raise funds to help pay my salary? Spirit chuckles heartedly about this knowing quite well that

I cherish a challenge. Of course, I immediately said yes and begin to work on the transformation that I first thought was about them, to realize it was going to be my life which transformed allowing others to follow or choose a different path. There has been about an equal split between those who chose to leave and those who remained, those who followed and are now leaders in their own right. This journey has been about consciousness, realizing what it means and radiating this awareness out into the world through demonstration and life activities.

Filled with certitude that this could change for the better I set my intentions and begin to imagine the good flowing to us. Within six months the cash was made available, I was paid in full and we hardly looked back. There are still struggles surrounding the increase of revenues to sustain the activity, but experience is on our side and we move forward with a greater ease and knowledge that we can do this. Once again Spirit has opened a pathway to experience life in the flow of abundance, strength and feeling good. With every experience I am guided to go deeper and reveal this thing called Life to practice the Principles of Religious Science as taught by Dr. Ernest Holmes in the Science of Mind. With each step of accomplishment, one creates an atmosphere of living the good life. Through an accumulation of success there is a willingness to explore new and different avenues of growth and living a principled life. Especially within a community that has felt deeply wounded and lost sight of hope or the possibility of reviving a sense of well-being.

Personally, during this time of evaluating where the Center was in its survival, I meet my current husband. At a time when I wasn't seeking a relationship, in order to be focused on the job at hand, there he was. It was as if he had been delivered on my doorstep. The ease and effortlessness that presented this relationship was phenomenal. Spirit knows full well my desires and wants and just when I needed an intimate, loving supportive being in my life, it happened. Once again, I smile at how this Divine Intelligence can demonstrate and manifest the perfect outcome, especially when we get the small self out of the way. Such is the writing of Ralph Waldo Emerson, The Over-Soul. (Emerson, 1945), "I am constrained every moment to acknowledge a higher origin for events than the will I call mine."

Renewed within the confines of my intimate life I gave my marriage vow on a promise to spend the next 60 years together in joy and exploration of life. Consciousness being the heart and love of all that is, I know this is doable. The path once chosen will forever unroll before us, if we are disciplined in keeping our intention and our focus to the chosen path. No one can foresee the turns and rises along the path but one can trust in the Divine Intelligence to provide our every need in a timely fashion when we remain open to receive. How simple this truth is and yet how complicated we strive to make it so. It appears that the human race has set out to test the very will of God in spite of having thousands of years in experience to show otherwise. Therefore, we continue to seek the urge deep within to uncover and reveal truth and to do so through trial and concerted effort. Looking toward the next 60 years, I chose the path of joy, love and wisdom. Requiring of myself to relax into the journey and move with each turn or twist in the same way a willow tree bends and flows with the passing wind. One way that I am assured will maintain my intention and focus is to find time and space to be in silence.

Silence is the practice of meditation, relaxation and release that opens the portals of the soul to allow the "still, quiet voice of Spirit" to speak directly to our conscious mind. Many have reached this point of silence in a most dramatic way where they are required to surrender to the Power Within as all exterior objects have fallen away. One definite example of this is the story "Conversations with God" by Neale Donald Walsch. (Walsch, 1996). With the crying of his heart drowning out all other sounds until finally he heard the voice of God. The voice was available within him for any question that he may be seeking an answer and patiently waiting for him to quiet his mind and ask. How often do we see someone randomly yelling out to no one in particular and question their sanity, perhaps they know more than we suspect? Living in the object world has led us to believe there is more power in things than within our own soul. Yet no matter how much we change the objects, the people, the environment we are still as unhappy or angry or hateful as we were in the beginning. All change must first come from within. We can talk to God, but we need to get very quiet and silent in order to hear the response. ❖

## Chapter One

# God Is All There Is

Re-labeling or re-framing the concept of God is often a major step for someone entering into the study of metaphysics. How we perceive this idea of the Infinite and Absolute will show the direction we are taking in the adventure of life. There is a question that I like to ask as I begin the morning: "Where does your heart live today?" Gratitude as the keystone to how we approach our daily life and understanding of things greater than our ego self will establish the tone of the day. To awaken and immediately become aware of something to be grateful for starts our thinking in the upward spiral of goodness. Goodness is God and there is little left for us to know about the Infinite. Our efforts to try and understand an Infinite and Immortal Beingness from the position of the human experience certainly will cause more confusion. Albert Einstein is quoted as saying that what he wanted was to know the Mind of God, everything else was just details. Defining God is an academic adventure that knows no limits and has been the foci of many a scholar, religious organization and meanings of war. Perhaps a different approach is to prove an existence in our life that works for us as the individual.

Can we talk to God? Do we talk to God? I'm wondering how often we stop and think about this conversation that is actually going on all the time? In a series of lectures in the 1930's, Ernest Holmes, the founder of Religious Science used this as one of his topics and has since been published under this title: *Can We Talk To God?*, (Holmes, 1992). Perhaps our approach is often as Dr. Holmes states more about how we talk at God. Either God is there or God is not. And if there is an Intelligence that is present then why not have a conversation that includes a reciprocal response.

Now, what it requires from someone who has not been in metaphysics, that has not been in the study of The Science of Mind©, (Holmes, 1938), that are coming from, a different belief; They have to do a major shift in their consciousness when we say something like, "Can we talk to God? Let's have a conversation with God." Because, first of all, they have to question, what is their belief about God, and if God is an entity, if God is something that is somewhere far beyond our reach or our comprehension, off into the heavens, out into the far edges of the universe or maybe beyond that, it might be a little difficult to consider that we could have a conversation with God.

Of course, there are people that we have seen on the streets that are having conversations with God, and many times we make the statement, "But by the Grace of God, there go I." I better not have that conversation with God because they might lock me up. You have to look at your belief. You have to look at what is your idea of God and begin there.

*Conversations with God,* (Walsh, 1996), by Neale Donald Walsch, who is having an extraordinary conversation with God about how his life is being played out in such great drama. Gee, wouldn't that be wonderful, that you could wake up one morning and just know that you were having this conversation. And in the movie about his life you realize that wasn't a simple process for him to get there. Not only was he experiencing this drama, but others would react to him out of their own pain and drama of life. It suggests that there is more to the idea of the Law of Attraction than most of us are keenly aware. When we begin to focus in on aspects of our life, our vibration becomes like a strong magnet and pulls into our experience even more of what we have focused upon. Simply put, if you focus on what is not working in your life, then more of this "not working" will show up. It is as if, my life is moving along, and it is not yet perfect. Not everything is absolutely the way that I think it ought to be. It is like the riches and the fame and the fortune and the princesses and princes or palaces or whatever is coming about, but maybe not in the time that I think they ought to, but it is moving along okay. And then all of a sudden, out of nowhere, everything that you had, everything that you thought you had, and everything that you thought you wanted was taken away from you. Where do you go?

How do I have a conversation with God and not get locked up as behaving psychotic? And I don't want to have that experience of I have to be so beaten down, I have to be so at the point of desperation that I can finally open up to the idea that the Presence is already here.

So, the message is that we don't have to go there. We don't have to have that dissolute desperation in order to understand that It is already here, that It is simply present right here, right now, and you get to make the choice. We need to have this conversation with God on a daily basis because It is already there, even when, we may not like what we see. We have the choice to change because we are all part of the One. We are shifting in consciousness our awareness and our idea about what is this thing called God. Some of us were brought up in that idea that It (GOD) is some place outside of us, that we are always looking outside of us, not only for the good but everything that is not working, we want to put blame on something outside of us. We want to put it all over somewhere, somebody, someplace, some thing, and the truth of the matter is It is all right here within us. It begins here, and It ends here, and It stays here, and It never leaves here. It is always right within us.

There is also this part of us that is what some call the "ego" part of us. When "ego" gets in the way and it has the tendency to twists things up. Have you ever had that feeling, it's like life somehow got twisted up someplace? That's part of the ego gone wild without discipline. All of this is me and I need to find a way to be inclusive with myself. I have to be able to be friends with myself. I have to be able to be in love with myself in order to have that experience and that expression of having a friendship or being in love with God. Because if It is already here, and I don't like what's here, then I can't have a friendship with God. So, I've got to make this all okay. There is no easy way to comprehend the wholeness of life. Life is the experience we have chosen from someplace deep within our soul.

There is an Absolute spiritual realm in which everything always is whole, perfect, and complete, always has been and always will be, and It will never change. And out of that, out of Itself, sitting there in this wholeness of everything being whole, perfect, and complete, said, "Wouldn't it be fun to have experience?" There is no experience in the Absolute because It just is. And so out of Itself It created because that's Its nature, to create. It created the universe, and It made it absolutely exactly what it is, already manifested, already made, and It is in this process of having the experience.

So, in this experience there must be form and from the thought of experience came human life. There are the animals, and there are the plants, and there are the trees, and there are the mountains, and there's the air, the fire and the light and all that has been created.

And there is human life, and human life has this ability to choose. And because Itself had determined that experience was what It was seeking, then It had to give it free choice. It had to give it free will. And so, it is out of that free will, and it is out of that free choice that we have created or co-created, if you will, everything that we are in experience of in our life.

So, this is what we wanted. You're here today because this is what you want. You are what you are today because this is what you want. Now, you may not have exactly thought of it in the way you think as when you are looking at a new automobile, "Well, I want air conditioning. This is important." However, we have made choices on a daily basis both individually and collectively that must eventually find an avenue of expression. We don't make conscious choices of everything that we have had and everything that we are going to do because some of it is a part of the evolution. Some of it is that part that has become automatic.

There are things that are automatic. These are things that we have created in the evolution of human kind to be an automatic response. They are moving along the way they are designed to be moving along. Then there are other things that we have decided that we need to really have a conscious choice in action. Now, the mistake or the error that we make is that we haven't really made a conscious choice of it. We have so many thoughts in a given day and without a discipline or focus of intention we randomly flip from idea to idea.

I grew up in a religion that said that there were a lot of things that were called "sin." And "sin" was about, as I understood it, the fear of God and the ability to take guilt over the top; that I was going to not do things in my life, one, either because I feared God, or two, I just felt so guilty that I wouldn't do it.

The more I learned and experienced the more this didn't work for me. I did it anyway and not only once but probably several times before I realized that it wasn't the way it was going to work for me. I now know, "sin" is an archery term that just means you missed the bull's-eye. It doesn't make anything wrong. It just means you missed the bull's-eye, and so you make corrections. You make a correction in order to hit the target. That's all it means, is to make a correction.

If you have ever flown on a jet, airplanes make corrections all the time. You think that when the plane leaves Los Angeles and it flies to New York that it goes on a direct path. This is not so. It's constantly changing altitude and attitude and its direction. It has to every now and then make a correction and bring itself back onto the path.

This is what we do in life. We get to correct the path, the direction in which we are going, the altitude of which we are moving, or maybe the attitude in which we have. Often times we need to correct our attitude. You can change your attitude with a 2 X 4 board on the side of the head, or you can change your attitude by simply making a new choice and moving into a more direct path.

So, we have the Absolute realm, the realm of Spirit, of which we are all are a part of. We are all spiritual beings having human experiences right here. And when we are finished with this, we move more into the Absolute. Everything is perfect just as it is. But in our experience of being humans, we have to have the experience, otherwise what's the purpose of being here? And if we are going to be here for an experience, then why not have fun with it? Why not enjoy it? This is why I had to give up guilt, in order to enjoy my experience. And I had to give up fear, even the fear of God, in order to have my experience. It was out of that that I realized that there is no heaven. Heaven is not about a location, it is an experience. The good thing in that is that there is no hell. You can experience all you want in your life, and you get to choose. Where do you want to go with it? Do you want to have the heaven right here and right now? That's what I understand when the master teacher Jesus said; Heaven is here right now, and hell is too. And it is your choice. You get to recreate your life, if you feel like you are a little bit too much over here and you want to be a little bit over there. You make that correction, and you make that choice.

Rev. Dr. Tom Costa shared a wonderful experience that he had; he told his story that, as a minister you are always looking for a line to demonstrate a teachable moment. You are always looking for something that you want to share. And as he was traveling someplace, and he had to go through the immigration or the passport checkpoint, and the agent there gave him this wonderful line. He said, "So where are you coming from?"

And he was like, "What a great one liner."

Where are we coming from? Where are you going? How long are you going to stay there? Isn't that true about life?

We should ask ourselves this question every day in our conversation with God because God is within you. God speaks to you in your own voice wherever you are. When you get up in the morning, you can ask yourself, "Where are you coming from? Are you coming from this place of hell? Are you coming out of that experience of life is not working?" And if it is not working for you, then you need to change. Okay, how do you change? Well, you have to look at your beliefs. You have to be willing — there is the keyword — you have to be willing to step forward and say, "I'm going to look at my beliefs." "Is there something I want to change in my life? Each morning create an activity as an opportunity to show up and begin to explore this idea that we can take our life someplace else.

There are so many tools available to you. You can read them. You can watch them. You can listen to them. You can participate in them. But you have to take the step. You have to be the one willing to do it. You are the one that has to open up and have that dialogue and that conversation with yourself. It doesn't have to be in public, and I highly suggest that it probably is not. You find a nice quiet place and begin to have that conversation. What is your belief? What is your belief in God? And if you believe that God is here within you, then you have already made the biggest step, and you can begin to move forward with that.

So, in the silence of your mind, just simply and graciously say good morning to yourself. Good morning, God. This is (your name). I welcome you into my Life fully and completely. I know that I am breathing; that my heart is beating; that the blood is flowing through my body because God is alive within me. And It is that very Presence of the Divine Spirit that flows through me, that creates the experience of my day. And now I am putting in my order of what I would like my day to be.

And just in the next moment, in the silence of your mind, make up that order. What is it that you would like this day to be? In my day I see peace. I see harmony. I see abundance and prosperity. How good it is that when we ask, and we listen, and we become open to receive, that the voice of God answers clearly, with certitude that every request has already been made so. Give us the eyes to see, the ears to hear, the life to experience, the wisdom to know. And we know this that it is done by the thoughts that we are creating. So carefully examine your thoughts, examine your beliefs, and choose the good ones. ❖

## Chapter Two

# *Creativity*

W here Does Creativity Come From?" Ernest Holmes in the "Creative Mind and Success", (Holmes, 1919) writes, "He (student of Mind) can create such a strong mental atmosphere of success that its power of attraction will be irresistible." Declaring that it is in the mind of the individual to create their success or whatever they desire to draw into their life.

In a series by Neville, who was a contemporary of Ernest Holmes, *Awakened Imagination*, he speaks to the idea that it is in the imagination we find creativity. It is interesting as he writes in here about the use of "imagination," the word. And how many words, often as we use them, that they sometimes begin to lose their whole meaning, or they bring out another meaning, and they no longer mean what we thought they meant.

So, when you begin to speak with people and talk and converse, and they start using words, you think, "What did they really mean?" What were they saying about me or something else, and was it really a compliment? Or were they just trying to find a way to slip it in under the door where I wouldn't notice and come about from the other side?

Imagination is one of those words. We can use imagination when we talk about, "It is just a figment of your imagination," or "You know, they are just caught up in their imagination." So, imagination is not necessarily what we might believe it to be. This was the way in which Walt Disney created a different world. We know that Disney is all about "imagineers." They take the word, and they use imagination in the way that we do in Science of Mind®, about that idea of creativity.

This whole idea of creativity, I struggled with for a long time. I always wanted to be somebody that was creative, and I love the arts. I have no talent in that area whatsoever. And so, for years, I would wander around and say, "As much as I love it, I just don't have a creative bone in my body." That's the affirmation I used about myself. And I would go forth, and I would struggle with this. My intimate relationships have been with artistic individuals.

Each one of them was an artist, and they created in the visual arts, and were very creative and very successful. And this was my way of living creatively through somebody else. But there was still this little nagging thing back behind me that said, "Where is my creativity? Where am I with that?" And I finally came into this realization that my creativity lies in a whole different realm.

I had a special focus ministry, Children's Treatment Center; I was the Executive Director for over 16 years. And there was my creativity. I found my passion. I connected to that. There was a part of me that said this was my passion and I was able to use it. I was able to create out of that something that was even a more expansive experience than I could have participated in any way around the visual arts as that was not my talent. That was not my gift. But I had a gift in another way to use.

Neville in his book *Awakened Imagination* quotes the artist William Blake. "Imagination is the very gateway of reality. Man is either the arc of God or a phantom of the earth and of the water. Naturally, he is only a natural organ subject to sense. Eternal body of man is the imagination that is God himself."

Man, in his nature state is of the physical senses. We have touch, smell and taste as our senses, physical senses. But the real eternal part of who we are is that of God Itself. And that is the point in which creativity emerges. We look at science, and how science has gone through this whole idea about left brain, right brain. I know that one of them is supposed to be this very creative part. And the other one is very linear, so one is linear, and one is creative but is that where creativity comes from?

The brain is just one of our organs. It is just one of the senses in which we use in order to allow for that expression of God to come into form and into reality. My understanding about quantum physics is that the potential of all is already made. Quantum physics talks about how form just pops in. There it is. It pops in. That happens out of our observation. It does that out of our thought and our thinking process. And that's how we create. That's how we create in our life. It is this, "Change your thinking, change your life," believing you have the ability — and you do. If you use your ability and your power that is already within you, then you can create absolutely anything and everything that you want in your life. Now, the caveat that comes with that is, be careful what you ask for.

Often, I teach in class about this idea of how to create your life. That you have to set your intentions for your life. And we talk about the difference between intentions and goals. Goals are the end result of what we out-picture, what we see. Intentions are channels of essence and the quality of God. Therefore, you want to move and be more of intentions. You want to hold the thought about the quality of God that you are looking for versus the picture that you might have. There is nothing wrong with creating a picture because what you can see you can create. You want to have some idea of what it is that you are seeking, or better, that you can reach for. Great athletes can visualize the performance within their mind. Now, it would be nice to say that everything in my life is perfect because I have created it as such. The truth of the matter is that we live in a world in which we are all interconnected. We are not alone. So, one individual does not hold responsibility with everything that is going on in the world right now. One can be a part of it, but cannot be held responsible for the entirety of it.

Draw your good into your sphere of influence.

When I realize I'm not responsible for everything that is going on in the world right now. I can have a part of it, and I can make a difference in it. And if I raise my consciousness to that higher level by using the power within me for good, then I can bring forth into the world a better place, a better experience. There are a couple of really strong motivators of why I want to make the world a better place. I want the world to be a better place because I have a grandson and a granddaughter. I want them to experience the joy and the beauty, the abundance and the love that I know is available, that I know I have glimpsed and I have experienced at different places and different times in my life. And I continue to call love forth, and I continue to try to bring more of this into my life. Knowing that there is never a limit, then others can also experience this life.

I want to continue to grow spiritually, mentally, emotionally, physically, in that idea of being able to live life creatively, to be able to fully express that which is my purpose. I have a belief that we are here in this experience as human beings just for that, to experience life, nothing more, nothing less. We get to choose at what level and at what degree we want to do that. I want to live my life fully every day to my greatest potential and possibility. And that means I have to reach out, and I have to step out, and I have to boldly go where others have not yet gone. Because it is only in that going out there and going past the edge that we begin to really feel the vibrations of life.

My friend George W. wrote a children's story, about a puzzle piece that struggled to get out of the box and starts moving around the playroom because it wants to find out where it fits in. Each individual is a part of the whole, a puzzle piece, and when you are here -- actually wherever you are, whoever you are with -- you make the picture complete. This right now is a complete picture. Using our creativity, we can rearrange our mind and fit in again with the whole picture of Life. Through our false beliefs and mistakes in life we feel that we are lost.

How can you be found, if you don't admit that you were lost? You already know where you are. You already know your experience and your place in life. And there is always something more. There is always something greater. Ernest Holmes says that life is about an upward spiral. It appears that we keep coming back around to those same issues and those same situations, "Oh, here I am again in relationship," or "Here I am again in that job," or "Here I am again." Look and see if you have not come to it again but at a higher level.

One of my first teachers in Science of Mind® was Reverend Marcia, who has been through a few marriages. She says that she can measure the growth of her spiritual advancement by the fact that she knows on one date what it used to take a whole marriage. It's the same situation, but we see it with new eyes. We have grown to a new level.

Creativity is in that space between inhale and the exhale, closer than even your breath is the presence of God because each and every one of us is an individualized expression in our own personality of that Divine Spirit, which I already know is whole, perfect, and complete; that all of us have already found our place in the puzzle, that we fit in perfectly, and that we know that we can have a greater experience in life just by the simple choice of calling upon that creative power, our imagination. And when we speak of imagination, we are not speaking of something, but we are speaking from something, that we imagine we are already there. We imagine that we are already in that experience. We are in the knowingness of our good.

In the next moment in our own mind's eye, when we begin to create and imagine what is that experience that we wish to have in our life, in our community. Is it a healing? Is it a greater sense of joy? Is it a better life, more prosperity, or abundance? Is it about love? We bring that image forward into our mind's eye. It might be a color. It might be a sensation. It might be a word. It may be a full- blown, video. However, it is that it comes to you; know that it is coming from within you. This is our potential. We step into it and embrace it. We are the Divine Expression. This is who we are. This is our joy and our beauty. This is our love and our understanding. Acknowledge it, embrace it and be it, then just simply let it go. Hold no attachment to it, and affirm that it is already made so and, so it is. ❖

## Chapter Three

# *Life Is*

The Autumn Equinox is about the constellation — the earth and all of the planets are moving into the constellation of Libra. And Libra is about balance. Growing up in Iowa, I know about seasons. I knew about autumn. The leaves begin to change color. The harvest was pulled, after which the community would create all kinds of celebrations.

Looking back into history and into ancient times, many of the tribes and the indigenous people would celebrate the harvest. It was a time of celebrating from their labor all of the fruits that they had gained. They were preparing for the winter season and awaiting a new season and a new life. It was a time and place to be held as sacred.

It is an opportunity for us to look at how our year has been, how has our life been showing up, and is there something that we want to harvest, bring in that which is nurturing us and nourishing us and supporting us and build the storehouse. It is a time when farmers plow under all of the old stuff that's no longer needed because it just goes back into the earth, and it gets regenerated in the spring for the next crop to come forward.

Life is like that too, Life is—abundant, dance, gratitude, challenging. Ernest Holmes, the founder of Science of Mind®, wrote a wonderful book in 1919 called *Creative Mind and Success*. In the very beginning of this he states, "Life is all there is." We have heard it stated, It is abundant,

It's beautiful, It's challenging. It's too short. It is everything. Life is all there is. If you haven't figured it out yet, if you don't get it that this is real, I am here to tell you that life is real. Everything about this is absolutely real. If we could separate all of the little camouflage that we have added onto it, we would come back to a point in which we would discover that life is in our awareness. It was in our allowing something to be a belief that opened the door for that challenge, that opportunity, that success, or that failure to come into life.

Because I don't believe any of us gets up in the morning and says, "Okay. Today I'm going to go out and fail. You know, I'm going to really make a mess of life today. I'm really going to see how many places I can mess up and stumble and really create chaos." But how often do we get up in the morning and we go, "Oh, I hope today is good. I don't want --" and then we start going into all of those things that look like, the chaos and the mess and that which we then create because we've believed that it is possible. And so, in that simple process, we've opened up for that possibility to come into our life.

As Ernest Holmes said in *The Creative Mind of Success,* (Holmes, 1919), "Life is all there is. It is a power of the universe, and It is changeless." Gravity is a power in the universe, and it doesn't change. We can use it, but it doesn't change. Man-made laws we can change. Man- made laws most of us find ways around it. We try to manipulate it. We try -- if there is not a police officer around, to believe we can go a little faster. I really don't need to stop at this stop sign because there is no other traffic here. So, we make those choices.

In life there is an Absolute Law that says, "Whatever you ask for, it is given." The Master Teacher Jesus says that it is done unto to you as you believe. If that's so, then what are you believing? If I believe that I can be poor, then that's what is going to come into my life because I've opened up for that possibility to come into my life. And I do it in so many ways when I walk around, and I start looking at all of the things that I don't have. Well, I must not be abundant because I don't have this, and I don't have that, and I don't have all that I want. And I start focusing on what I don't have. Well, I asked for a million dollars, but it didn't come. Right there I changed the thought. The universe is like, make up your mind. You say you want a million dollars, but then you go, "Oh, well, I am probably not worthy of it. I'm probably not deserving of it." Life is, and you get to make it up. You get to co-create it. You do so by the process in which way your thought pattern goes. So, it's about changing your beliefs.

Try to sit down and say, "What do I believe in? What is it that I am absolutely convinced, without a shadow of a doubt that I can hold true, that this is what I want my life to be?" And then when I know that and when I know that as I have the power to create my life, and I focus on it, and I stay there, and every time the thought that comes up that looks like something less than or lack or limitation I go, oh no, huh-uh. It's not the truth because I no longer believe in that. Because I believe that I am abundant and prosperous and whole and complete in every way. That is knowingness, and it is not about a miracle.

I believe that the man, Jesus, was not about miracles. He was about something that he knew. When he walked in and he saw somebody that couldn't walk, he didn't go, "Oh, look at that poor man. He can't walk. I should do something about that." He walked in and said, "I absolutely know there is a power in the universe that if you choose, if you are willing, ready, and able, that you will walk." Because there is nothing in the universe that denies that it is available to you. And because the people were able to get that conviction from him, they got up and walked. Jesus is not the only person that has done this. It happens all the time. There are people today that are walking around here that are creating their life in every way that they want to. It shows up right here in my Center/church. People come in and say, "You would not believe the wonderful thing that happened to me." I say, "Yes, I will. Just tell me."

Now, if I happen to be something that guides you to that, if I happen to be something that illuminates that and says, "It's possible," then I'm willing to be that person to somehow stimulate, this idea that you can have in your life that greatness and that abundance and that prosperity and that health and that beauty, but I don't do it. I do it for me because I'm responsible and accountable to my life, and I change my life. I have no power over yours. People may want to give me power over their life, and I keep saying, "I don't want it." I do not want to have power over your life. I want you to have the power of your life because life is, and that's all there is.

We have the opportunity here to be in the experience of life. Choose it wisely. And if you haven't chosen it so wisely on all of the things along the way, you get to choose again right here, right now. You can begin to make a new choice.

The way we do that is that we have to reevaluate what we are thinking about. What is our thought process? It is all mental. Everything spiritual is mental. It is all in the mind. It really is absolutely in the mind. This was what Ernest Holmes was saying, if you can convince yourself that it is the truth, then it absolutely will be.

And so how do we convince ourselves that it is the truth? We have the tools of affirmations and prayer. The prayer work that the practitioners and the ministers have been trained in is scientific — it's nothing magical. It is about that confirmed conviction that it is absolutely the way that I want my life to be. And if I'm out there in the world, and most of us are, day in and day out — there's a lot of people out there in the world that don't want you to have that because that doesn't match up with their belief. They believe that you really have to suffer, and they want you to suffer because it supports their suffering. The story sounds like; "If I believe in suffering, then you have to suffer too because otherwise it is not fair".

There are people that are absolutely wealthy in the most devastating of times because they don't buy into the story. When there is a mass economic depression, it is because many choose in some manner or behavior that buys into that story and goes, "Oh, it is really real, and everybody is going to lose their money." And there are a group of people over here that are saying, "Not my story. Don't want to hear it. Don't want to be a part of it." And they continue to amass millions while everybody else looks at not amassing the millions. See how you have to support your belief. Believing they are wrong in making money because you don't have any, and you want everybody else to be in your suffering with you is not an affirmative prayer on life.

We make all kinds of excuses. We make all kinds of justifications about why we are not over here in this prosperous group. The ones who succeed all report of success, "because I believed I could, I could." In the last semester of the practitioners' studies a student was complaining, "There's no work. There's no work. There is no work." And she wasn't getting any work. I said, "You've got to change that." And now she is, she reports, "I got too much work. I got too much work. I've got too much work. I've got to reevaluate. I want the right and perfect job." That's exactly how powerful this is, and that's how it works. I want to talk about it. I want us to be excited about it because that's what becomes contagious. In the same way that people will attract wealth to them — and you can put any word in here — health, beauty, abundance — they will attract it to them because they believe that it can be.

And everybody that doesn't want to believe it is going to negate it and if you let them have power in your life then it attracts negativity. How many times have you had that wonderful idea only to have someone negate the idea? Reverend Diane Harmony talked about this in her book, "The Five Gifts for an Abundant Life", to have had that wonderful idea and shared it with another. You knew it was the next greatest invention in the world, and the first person you said it to, they said, "Huh-uh. It isn't going to happen." And you said, "Oh, okay." And you didn't follow through, and you didn't do anything with it. What's that about, giving away your power to someone else? When you need to come back within and find the power within you and declare that it is so, and know that it is so and say, "This is my power." Now, I'm not one that is willing to go out and to share with a lot of people, the things that I want to bring into my life because I don't want the naysayers shooting it down before I have the opportunity to get anchored in it. That's when I find that quiet time, that's when I take those opportunities to sit in the stillness, so that I can be in my conversation with God, so that I know that I am fully supported in what it is that I want. We all talk to God all the time because whether you know it or not, It is you. It is in you. It is the life that you are. It is the breath that you are breathing. It is the planet on which you are standing. Because life is all there is, and that's what God is. It is the First Cause of all that is. When you get that, when you understand it to the depth of your soul, then you too will be able to bring into your life experience that which you are seeking so often, so deeply. But you must be convinced that that is the truth and hold to it and not allow others to get in your way. How easy it would be, if you picked up a newspaper and read it from cover to cover and believed that everything in there was your experience. Whoa, that's scary. That's why I just kind of like scan through it. "Don't believe that. Don't want that in my life." Not that it's not there, not that it's not real. It is all real. This is real. And yet the physicists will tell you that it is only real because you believe that it is, and that in actuality there is a great deal of space in a solid wall. It is in that space and in that vastness that God exists in all time and in all places, and It responds all the time instantaneously.

So, your life is just that expression of what you have asked for, what you have opened up to, what you have allowed, and more often than not it has been unconscious. You heard somebody say something, you read something someplace, and you allowed that to become a part of your process. Well, it must be true.

Dr. John Waterhouse in his book *The Five Steps of Freedom,* (Waterhouse, 2003), tells about the story that he lived and grew up mostly in Florida, and now he's in North Carolina. At the time of this book he was traveling, and he had heard on the way home that it was snowing. He was so excited because he really loves snow now that he's moved there because it was not his experience. So, he was waiting to get home, so he could see the snow, and when he landed, and he was looking out the window. He said "Oh, there's snow." And the guy next to him said, "No. There's no snow." He said, "Oh, wait a minute. I'm a grown intelligent man. There is snow out there." And the man said, "No. There is no snow." "Well, I heard it -- I heard it on the news."

And the man next to him said, "Just before we left, I called my wife, and she said we had an unusually warm day today, and all the snow has melted." And he looked again, and there was no snow. He had so convinced himself that there was snow on the ground. That's what he saw because that's what he wanted.

And that's exactly how it works, every time. When you hear something, if you take it in, and if you believe that it is true, then it will be true. We see it all the time. And so, if that is in actuality the way it works, then consciously we can now begin to change that. I no longer want to accept that story of lack and limitation. I no longer want to accept that story of disease and illness. I'm now moving into the vibration of the center of who I am that says that I am whole and perfect and complete, and that my life is abundant. It is whole. It is healthy. It is wise. It is everything that I want and then some. And then I need the support to stay there because all of us will find ourselves leaning back into the negativity. So, we need to find the support. That's what the classes and workshops and the seminars and the mid-week service that we do to support us, to come together as like-minded people and say, as I look out at you, I see perfection in each and every one of you, always. Everyone here, right now, is perfect. And as long as you can hold onto that, then that's what will show up in your life.

Is there an experience you want to change? Is there a condition that you want to move out of your life? Is there a greater good that you want to experience? Within your own mind imagine what that is. When we are consciously aware of the power we wield, we are free to live in our wholeness, expressing and experiencing the Divine Love that we are. Using daily affirmations saying; I live in a world created by Love. Love is what I am, and all that I think say and do, Love is what I am. Before me, behind me, around me, inside me, Love is what I am. I am filled to overflowing and clear in my knowing that Love is what I am. ❖

## Chapter Four

# *Demonstrating Success*

Is life good or not?

There is always that moment when you walk up, and you say, "Am I going to be in alignment? Am I going to be in joy? Am I going to be in harmony? Am I going to be in love?" We have the opportunity to be whatever it is that we want to be. Out of your awareness, out of your consciousness, out of your willingness to show up and be a member of life, then we will demonstrate the success of who we are. Success is just an outcome, and we have labeled it good or bad. Outcomes are always the expression of how we use the Law. The founder of Science of Mind®, Ernest Holmes, said, "There is a power in the universe, a power for good, and it is available to each and every one of you."

Whether you know it or not, you are using the Power, you are using the Law every moment of every day in every conscious thought or unconscious thought that you have. And the Law responds, and the only way It can respond is with that resounding "Yes." When you are walking around, and you are tired and troubled, and you are talking about the burden and the story and whatever is going on, the universe says, "Yes, and I will give you more of it." If you want to experience how poor you are, the universe will be abundant in its expression of poverty. You will see it everywhere. In fact, that's all you will experience because that's the story you are telling. We need to change the story. We need to recreate and build the new story.

Here is an example that I use to demonstrate on how to change the story. When I arrived at my new position in the desert and people were saying to me, during the summers, everybody goes away. Nobody stays in the desert during the summer." And I'm thinking, what a fool I was because I signed a lease for a whole year. I have to stay here. My goodness, why didn't somebody tell me that we all leave in the summer? So, I changed the story. I said, "It's not my story. What I know is that summertime in the desert is fun, and I'm staying. And what I know is that there are others that live here too, and they are going to stay. We will have a full house." And I explicitly said to those people that as you go wherever you decide you are going, if you want to come back, you need to make reservations because I'm filling the seats. A greater number of people remained, and the congregation grew during the summer months. I am thankful for that, and I appreciate those who realized a new way of being. And that was the new story. And that's all it took was just to change the story. And it became manifest.

I am here to demonstrate the power of creativity that we have within us, that ability to change Your story so that Your outcome, your success is something that we can call good. The Law provides that there is always an outcome. Whether you label it good or bad is your perception. And if you go within and look about, what have you been saying? What thoughts have you been thinking? How have you been behaving? That's what gets created in your life. So, who's responsible for your life?

It is your life, and you get to create it. If you are not satisfied, if you are not fulfilled by the demonstration, by the success that you are creating in your life, then as we say, "Change your thinking, change your life."

Change your thinking, change your life. And it is a tough thing to stop and reflect upon what one is thinking. Because absolutely that's the way it works. So, what we think and we sometime call as miracles, it's just the movement of Spirit within each and every one of us always, every moment. And even if we somehow haven't figured out the exact words that we want to use, to set our intention or to set our prayer signals the Universal Mind that we are ready to change for the better. It's about being real. Speak the word as you know it because in the Mind of the Divine, It already knows. It already knows what's perfect. The Divine knows exactly what is the best, the best time and the best moment. Our job is to be present, to be conscious, and to be willing to receive.

So many of us block it from right there. I know what I want. I know exactly the dollar amount that I want in my checking account. I know the car that I'm looking for. I've got the house on my bulletin board. I've got the picture of the car on my bulletin board. I know exactly what it is that I want, but I don't know that I'm worthy enough. I don't know that I worked hard enough. I don't know that I've prayed enough, or I have used the right words for it. You just erased it because in that is your treatment. "I don't know. I'm not worthy enough." And the universe says instantaneously, "That's what you get, what you ask for." That's why you have to look at your thinking and your thoughts, and you have to be consciously aware of where it is that you are going.

When you find yourself going back to the story, you need to remind yourself that the story "was," and you are now in the "is." There is only this moment. And this moment. And this moment. The presence of God is now, right now. And the more you can keep yourself mentally in the now, the greater demonstration of your success.

That is the power of creativity. That is the power that is available within each and every one of us, all the time, everywhere. It doesn't make any difference whether you are in the desert or you are in the mountains or you are on the way to the moon. It is right now. Everything in this manifest universe has already been created in Divine Order and we have the choice to freely reveal our experience.

Your experience of how you want to perceive it is up to you. And if you are willing to stay in the good, if you are willing to stay in the awareness, if you are willing to stay in the consciousness that you are the I Am, then you will create your life in a way that is absolutely the demonstration of the greatest success.

This is our opportunity where we get to go within. We get to sit in the stillness and the quiet. If it feels right, you can just simply close your eyes, not because anything is going to happen but because it blocks out some of the distractions that are going on and around and about us. And these distractions are just the activity of God because it never stops. It is always in that upward spiral. It is always in that moment of creation. That which I call "God" is the creator. Each of us as an individualized expression of that Divine Spirit influences and co-creates the life experience that we have.

So right now, in this moment, in this quiet and stillness, in the pleasantness of being here and being present, what is your greatest intention for this day? What is your desire for this moment and this day or this week or this lifetime? What is the good that you would like to call forth and manifest, to declare as yours right here and right now?

We go into our imagination because there, just as children do, we create the reality of our world that we know is whole, perfect, and complete. Begin to envision that. And when you have a picture of what it looks like in the material, then underscore that with the quality of God that signifies and illuminates.

Is it about Love? Is it about Abundance? Perhaps it is Beauty or Wisdom or Truth? What is that quality? Perhaps it is just pure gratitude that you have for what you have right now. We focus on that quality of God. Perhaps we seek the kingdom of heaven first, and then all things shall follow. The prosperity and the wealth that you are seeking, the relationship, the right job, the career, the decision, the clarity, the understanding, all of that comes forth, and all of it comes regardless of which quality of God that you focus on because they are all one, and they all follow within.

Choose one, and then hold that in the mind of your heart. See it as that vibration that is resonating throughout your entire being. It fills your body, your soul, your mind. It becomes the essence of who you are. Just as I know that the sun shines each day, there is nothing I have to do in order to make that happen. It has already been set by that Divine Spirit which I know as God.

So, as I declare my intention, and as I know for you that your intention is absolutely for your highest good, I just simply surrender into the Power and Presence within. I call it good. I bless it, and I know that is so.

Determine what it is that you want to label as success? What is it that you want to bring into your life? What is the good that you want to experience more of? And then stay open and willing to receive it in its right and perfect place and time and not try to get into, "There is something I have to do about it." Because once you have set the intention, the Law has already put into motion everything that needs to happen in order for that to come forth.

Be in an attitude of gratitude right now, knowing that it is so. And whenever your mind starts to go someplace else, you say, "That's the way, and right now I Am, and It is." ❖

## Chapter Five

# The Law

## POTENTIAL & PURPOSE

Reading *The Seven Spiritual Laws of Success* by Deepak Chopra, (1994), he offers a simplified writing drawn from his Eastern Tradition of Indian Hinduism and The Vedas or Hymns of Praise and knowledge. I could have chosen any number of New Thought books that deal with The Law: The Four Laws of Prosperity, Working with the Law, The Law of Mind, Dynamic Laws of Healing, Love and Law, The Law and The Word and my all-time favorite, The Law according to Michael!

Ah, you laugh, I googled it and there is an article titled; The Law (according to Michael Dinowitz) Part 1, Cold Fusion set authority. Cold Fusion is another topic on Energy; I'm working with the idea of Spiritual Energy, which may be as difficult to describe as Cold Fusion.

Deepak gives us a basic concept of Law as we use it here in The Science of Mind teachings. "Law is the process by which the unmanifest becomes the manifest; it's the process by which the observer becomes the observed; it's the process by which the seer becomes the scenery; it's the process through which the dreamer manifests the dream." Simply stated Law is the way It works. Within our teaching symbol we identify law in the middle of the triune circle. The unmanifest working its way into the manifest. Ministers and Practitioners have all been students of this understanding of The Law. Each is deputized as having passed the Law exams and receiving their Licensure.

Dr. Ernest Holmes in the Science of Mind Text has nearly 200 entries regarding the Law. In the glossary he states, There is only One Law. Our misuse of this makes it appear that there are many laws. Whatever we think, believe in, feel, visualize, vision, image, read, talk about, in fact, all processes which affect or impress us at all, are going into the subjective state of our thought, which is our individualized us of Universal Mind.

*Law is the process or the way Spirit works in the Universe.*

Before there was existence, even before there was non-existence there was the Infinite, Timeless and Perfection. What should we call this that is the Source and First Cause? This Power of invisibility which through Its' own Intelligence brought forth the manifest Universe and keeps it alive and forever expanding. What should we call this that billions of years ago set in motion an activity that has placed our planet in perfect order and balance within the solar system. What should we call this that has created galaxies beyond our comprehension, all in perfect order and has also designed the order and life of every ladybug or butterfly? What should we call this that moves through every life whether it is plant, animal or person and how do we explain the way It works? Well, you can't name It. You can't define It and you can't even know It by using a finite and limited form to understand and explain an unlimited and infinite Life. Ever since we have tried to label the unknown, to define the unlimited to put in some box the idea of God, we have created chaos, anger, war and hate, as we tried to prove our self right or superior to others.

Only when we began to understand our unity and connectedness with all that is will we truly began to experience peace, balance and order in our lives. Even the words and the way I am expressing here is limited and likely to cause discomfort or disorder for someone, somewhere in sometime. However, the hope is, the light is, the illumination is in the creative process that is our nature and in-dwells within everyone and is available for our use. This is the law. We don't have to fully understand this Power to use it. Most of us don't understand the automobile, yet we use it. We don't fully understand the computer and we use it. We don't understand jet airplanes and we use them. We really don't understand electricity and, yet we use it everywhere all the time. We have placed our trust and confidence in the skills and talents of others without hesitation. Every time we flip the switch expecting the light to illuminate we trust that it works. We turn the key to our car and expect it to work. We open the refrigerator with expectancy that the milk is chilled, and the vegetables are kept fresh. Trusting, of course, that we put milk and vegetables in the refrigerator. How convenient life has become for us as we surrender and trust in the workmanship and talents of others to bring us what we want and when we want it. We have been conditioned, trained and disciplined by every conceivable external force in our life to surrender our happiness, our well-being and our self-esteem to some object outside of and otherwise not a part of our true self. As devastating as the economy appears to be, as abusive and degrading as one human being can be to another, as manipulative and deceiving individuals, corporations or nations can deliver one onto another, when death calls forth our physical body there is only one that will be called to answer.

*How do you use The Law, The Perfect Power Within?*

As he fell to the assassins' bullet, Mahatma Gandhi murmured, oh God! When his body succumbed to the harsh crucifixion, Jesus spoke, forgive them for they know not what they do! How will we answer when it is our time to surrender this physical temple? The meaning of Easter is not about the death and crucifixion; it is about the resurrection and new life. This is not about a form of religion. This is not about some story of redemption or the life of one man who may or may not have lived and died over two thousand years ago. This is about hope. It is about life eternal. It is about the life each one of us is living this day, this moment, right now. It is about each and every person, every life and the inter-connectedness that we are to a greater Whole.

It is not necessary for us to know or understand what the wholeness is, but we do need to understand that It is, and we are a part of it. Fenwicke Holmes, an older brother to Ernest, wrote daily lessons and Treatments in Mental and Spiritual Science in 1919, titled, *The Law of Mind in Action* (Holmes, 1919). He wrote, "There is one law supreme to this system of life. We speak of it as the method by which spirit passes into manifestation. Our happiness and success in life are measured by the degree to which either consciously or unconsciously we are obedient to the requirements of this law. It is the activity of Creative Mind, neither good nor bad, by which we create our own heaven and our own hell. It is the secret of all tragedy and all comedy. It is the truth that once you know it, it shall set you free."

The source of all creation is pure consciousness, pure potentiality seeking expression from the unmanifest to the manifest. And when we realize that our true Self is one of pure potentiality, we align with the power that manifests everything in the universe. Deepak gives the first law of success as the Law of Pure Potentiality. The Power within us that gives us our very breath, our life is this potential, unlimited and eternal. The conscious use of spiritual practice on a daily and hourly use in your mind will bring you to a greater awareness, a stronger alignment with the Power of the Universe. In *Growing the Positive Mind,* (Larkin, 2008), Dr. Larkin explains and interprets this as your Vibe Core: Knowing what you want, believing, really believing that you are going to receive it and stay open to the potential ways in which it can come into your life. Each of us selects the law under which we will live. We do not make the Law; but we decide which law we will obey. The citizen lives under civil law which he has helped make or has elected to live under it by choosing the State or Country to live in. The soldier is under the military law, the seaman is under the law of the sea. The physician submits to the law of medicine. The fearful trembling soul elects to live under the law of chances. The pessimist chooses to live under the law of the cloud; the optimist under the law of the sun. I live in the world of mind and spirit and will obey its laws. I have my being in a world where I control my own conditions. I exist in the heart of the Infinite.

*What law will you live under today?*

Anyone can create a process to help remind them of the law. Using foil or purchase a badge at the local toy store to make a shiny star. Consider what law you wish to declare and write this on the star. Here are some to consider: ABUNDANCE – BALANCE – BEAUTY – FREEDOM – JOY – LOVE – ORDER – PEACE – POWER – UNITY – WISDOM – WHOLENESS. Choose one or pick your own. Later you can write or stick a new note on your star to remind you through the week.

Today let me choose to live under the highest law of being, and let me go on in perfect security. I will keep my law and my law will keep me. I will obey my law and my law will obey me. Let me not forget that I make my world by the thoughts I think. My law today is love, faith, prosperity and truth. I look expectantly into my future for I am today sowing the seed for my future harvest, and it is good. I rest in peace and faith. I trust in God; His Law is Love.

One can create a week of affirmations to remind them of the law they are choosing to live by.

> *I know that God is Life.*
> *I know that God is Love.*
> *I know this Life and Love are in me.*
> *I know the power of faith in me.*
> *I feel the confidence of Love in me.*
> *I receive this Life and Love in gratitude.*
> *I give joyful thanks.*

## *Giving – The Law of Cause and Effect*

To run around trying to "fix" your world with the consciousness that produced the problem will only aggravate the situation even more. To change your world, you must change your awareness and expand your consciousness. To start this change, consider the following affirmative statement:

> *I am the Spirit of Infinite Plenty individualized.*
> *I am boundless abundance in radiant expression.*
> *I am a mighty money magnet.*
>
> *I am wonderfully rich in consciousness.*
> *I now realize my plan for abundant living.*
> *I feel love in my heart and know it is God. And*
> *So It Is!*

Fenwicke Holmes, *The Law of Mind in Action,* (Holmes, 1919), writes, "There is one law supreme to this system of life. Our happiness and success in life are measured by the degree to which consciously or unconsciously we are obedient to the requirements of this law." It is the law we cannot break, but we can be broken by our misuse of the law. It is the law by which "as you sow, you also shall reap". It is done unto you according to your belief. It is the basis of the Law of correspondence; it is the law of Cause and Effect.

All law is the activity of the Creative Mind. It is the very process by which the invisible becomes visible. I believe in the Creative Mind. Simply stated, I believe in God. Not just any God, this is not the God my parents presented. This is not the God that was painted on the church ceiling of my childhood. This is not the God by which others have interpreted in Scriptures, books or movies like George Burns or Jim Carrey. This Creative Mind or this God cannot be defined as that would create limits to something that is limitless. I also believe that the way it works is the law. Absolute, all powerful and always present. I accept and use the term law because it helps me to understand It and the more I can learn to understand It the more I can use the law to create the life of abundance, goodness, joy and happiness. I have no desire to give up this life any time soon. I also want to live the greatest life potential that I can imagine; therefore, my intention is to continue exploring the depths of my consciousness and reaching for an ever-expanding experience of joy and happiness.

Now what that does is attract me into groups, situations, friends and Centers for Spiritual Living filled with like-minded people. Notice I said like-minded, not the same mind, but like minded. This is our individualized mind I am referring to. Creative Mind is the One Mind, It is the Universal Mind and can only be One – Whole, Perfect and Complete. The individual mind is how each of us plays out our personal life. So, in that sense we can be like-minded and have the experience of a separate life.

The way in which we use our mind in the discipline of obedience to the Law is the way our life will out picture. Ernest Holmes wrote in the *Science of Mind* book, "Prosperity is the out- picturing of substance in our affairs. Everything in the Universe is for us. Nothing is against us. Life is ever giving of Itself. We must receive, utilize and extend the gift. Success and prosperity are spiritual attributes belonging to all people, but not necessarily used by all people." Simply stated the Law is there as a natural part of who we are. The use, the non-use or the miss-use of the Law is our individual choice. When we become so set on being independent, going our own way, trusting in only the physical world that we can see, touch, hear, smell or taste, we miss the opportunity to place our trust in God, in The Law and become obedient to the ever-flowing grace of Creative Mind.

Deepak Chopra lists the second spiritual law of success as the Law of Giving. The Cosmic Law of the Universe is that it is forever in the dynamic exchange of energy, a constant ebb and flow of physical universe within the harmonic field of existence. Life can be compared to the rising of the tide. With each successive approach of the ocean wave it jumps a little farther up and then recedes waiting upon the next wave to carry it a little further. This continues in the manner of rise and fall, forward and rest until finally it reaches that peak of highest ground and then recedes to reform and return another day. The tide follows the law. Obediently, respectfully it returns day after day, year after year with no concern other than to play the purpose for which it is meant to be. If we are made in the image and likeness of Divine Spirit, then it would suggest we are meant to be of the nature of Spirit, to be giving and receiving, the circulation of life. The Truth and The Law as described in *The Abundance Book* (Price, 1987) by John Randolph Price demonstrates the very principles that have been revealed over ages of time by the great thinkers.

Every relationship is one of give and take. Giving engenders receiving, and receiving engenders giving. What goes up must come down; what goes out must come back. In reality, receiving is the same as giving, because giving and receiving are different aspects of the flow of energy in the universe. And if you stop the flow of either, you interfere with nature's intelligence.

The Law of Giving is the most powerful way to receive what you want. If you desire more joy in life, then give joy. If you want more time, then give of your time. To give love is to receive love. Give it unconditionally and it will return as such. Give it with attachments and conditions and you will be bound by the very same attachments. Doing this in the silence, through the power of your thought is the greatest way to give without expectation.

As a process one can try this example. Think of something wonderful and joyful that you want. Love or joy or happiness or prosperity. Now remain in the silence and turn within and begin to mentally know for others that which you so desire. See it, feel it and in your mind's eye realize that they are receiving this gift multiplied in their life. No conditions, no expectations, no words, just powerful thoughts of good. Using this as a daily practice, or before entering a meeting or conference and I believe one will experience a higher level of fulfillment and satisfaction within the activity.

# FIVE - The Law

## *Effort, Intention & Detachment*

Our basic Principle in this philosophy, this faith, this way of Life we call The Science of Mind is simply; God is all there is, manifested in all creation as self-existent First Cause. There is only One Power and It flows through, as and is every being and every particle of the manifest and unmanifest universe. We are because God is.

Loosely defined, *the Seven Spiritual Laws of Success,* by Deepak Chopra can be stated as such: **1.** The Law of Pure Potentiality; Creation seeking expression from the unmanifest to the manifest. **2.** The Law of Giving; Giving and receiving is the flow of energy in the universe. **3.** The Law of Cause and Effect; Every action generates a force of energy that returns in like kind. **4.** The Law of Intention and Desire; In every Intention and Desire is the mechanics for its fulfillment. **5.** The Law of Detachment; Freedom from past conditions leads to the field of all possibilities. **6.** The Law of Purpose in Life; I have a unique gift and talent to give to the universe. **7.** The Law of Least Effort; Harmony, joy and love is the Nature of the Universe.

The Law of Least Effort defined by Deepak Chopra as "do less and accomplish more" is preceded with a description of nature at work. Claiming that as we observe nature we will learn effortlessness. His explanation goes like this; Grass doesn't try to grow, it just grows, Fish don't try to swim, they just swim. Flowers don't try to bloom, they just bloom. Birds don't try to fly they just fly.

Well I thought about this and started to think in that deep wonderful way that my mind goes. What was my observation of nature in my life experience. There are many very knowledgeable individuals, both past and present that suggest we can observe and learn from nature. In fact, most of the sciences that we study and seek out for knowledge are based on the study, observation and research of nature. What are we learning and observing in this study of nature? There are volumes of great knowledge stored in libraries, in books, in papers written throughout the ages, now we fill up tapes, cd's and hard drives. We have collected more data and information from one satellite probe to Mars that even a well-designed team of highly intellectual scientist will be able to decipher within their lifetime. Our children's children will be sorting through that information a hundred years from now. And it doesn't stop, it just keeps on coming. Once we believed the earth was flat and individuals were imprisoned, tortured and executed for believing otherwise.

*What have we learned through our observation of nature?*

Our prisons are overcrowded, torture is headline news and executions are at an all-time high worldwide. We know the rules change across time and space. Everyone seems to accept that planet Earth is not flat, probably more egg shaped than round but for convenience we build models that are perfectly round and downsize Greenland so it all fits nicely. Even if someone wants to declare the world is flat, we don't torture or execute them. We might try to get them on medication, but otherwise we just walk away. Yet, we have come up with some very clever and unique systems to otherwise create our opportunities through Race, Color and Creed. Easily plotting them out as Nationalism, Patriotism, Individualism or Religion. Not so different from the ancient imprisonment, torture and execution. Definitely more sophisticated, massive and secretive.

*What have we learned through our observation of nature and our fellow man?*

Growing up in farm country there was great opportunity to observe nature undisturbed. As I recall my childhood there wasn't the amount of distractions that I enjoy as an adult. Watching the grass grow in nature, as Deepak states, was for me a daily ritual. Not a lot else to do. Some days I would lay in the backyard trying to visibly see the moment when grass would grow. Usually, nothing happened. I would discover some bugs crawling around or ants building a tunnel or maybe drifting up to watch the clouds create a design in the sky. Looking back, I realize I could travel the Universe. Moving beyond any limitation of time or space I had a sense of freedom that was only limited by my imagination. There was also the limit of my Dad calling us in for dinner.

*What are we learning from this observation of nature?*

When it was my turn to mow the lawn, I learned that grass grows faster and thicker than at other times. I also learned it doesn't necessarily grow without effort. It would push itself up out of the soil, and that was effort. It would grow in the crack of the sidewalk, the driveway and even in the middle of the street. That was effort. I saw a lot of effort in nature. If you have ever observed plants growing, they don't just bloom. They extend out in all directions; some parts dig down deeper in the soil, seeking nutrients and moisture. Other parts explode upward and outward seeking sunlight and air. A blossom emerges out of a bud, moment by moment, day by day, stretching pushing and growing until it fully expresses its beauty and magnificence. All of this is tremendous effort, expending energy gained from the nutrients and the sunlight and the air.

*What are we learning from nature?*

Birds don't just fly, there is a tremendous expenditure of energy and effort. Having developed within an egg shell the chicks must chip and probe the shell seeking to crack it open in search for nutrients, light and air. Feathers and bones and muscle have to be developed. All this is energy and effort. Flying doesn't just happen. Have you ever seen a new born chick attempt to fly? Watch a tiny bird attempt to fly from the nest, and it often results in a not so graceful earth landing.

*What are we learning from our observation of nature?*

Animals, humans included, have been birthing their offspring throughout our existence. My daughter was unexpectedly born at home at 2 AM. I was also privileged to be in the delivery room at my grandson's birth. These required a tremendous amount of energy and effort. Especially for the mothers.

*What are we learning from nature?*

Here is some of what I've learned. Grass left alone will grow in every direction possible. However, it reaches a certain height and stops. Extreme cold, heat or dryness and it dies. So why bother cutting it? My Dad never saw the logic in this, and so, I mowed the lawn. Birds eventually learn to fly, and fish take to swimming as naturally as babies take to breathing. Interference happens at every level of life experience on Earth. Grass without nutrients and light won't grow. Fish over caught or in polluted water will become extinct. Birds that learn late to fly are subject to predators and babies sometimes do not survive the birth process. All of this has gone on since time existed and will most likely go on for some time immortal.

*What have we learned from our observations and study?*

The Law of Least Effort is not about "do nothing", and is more about making a choice of non-resistance. Mahatma Gandhi taught and practiced non-violent resistance. Each year from January through April I observe a period of non-resistance marking the anniversary date of the assignation of Mahatma Gandhi and Dr. Martin Luther King, Jr. My intention and effort are to focus within my life to be in a mental attitude of acceptance. This is not about doing nothing; it is about accepting people, situations, circumstances and events as they occur. Each moment is the culmination of all the previous moments. IT IS, because the entire UNIVERSE IS AS IT IS IN

THE MOMENT. Nothing I do will change this moment. It is as it is. I accept it. What I can do is make choices that will change the next moment, and the next moment and the next.

Far too many individuals are expending enormous amounts of energy and effort trying to change past moments in time. This is a waste of energy and effort. Focus on what you desire for the next moment and live as if it were so. The thoughts, the ideas and our mind are the place to spend our energy and our effort, creating the next moment in joy and happiness.

Here is a story about how we live in the past moments: "The old man shifted the load of wood from his back to the ground. It made no sound on the deep carpet of pine needles. Shivering, he sat down on a rotten log to rest his withered legs. Here he was in the middle of the forest and it was fast getting dark. *Why*, he whined aloud, should an old man like myself be forced to carry heavy loads of wood for younger, richer men to burn? Why? Oh, I wish Death would deliver me from this miserable existence and this burden of wood! To his astonishment, black-clad Death appeared instantly before him. What can I do for you, sir? The man asked pleasantly, fingering his sickle. Shocked at the sight of Death so close, the old man muttered; "Just... er, just help me up with my burden again." How quickly he changed his mind at the sight of Death so close upon him. Awkwardly and randomly wishing for things we do not want or have not thought out will allow for the idea of chaos and disorder to enter our life.

*What have we learned in our study of nature?*

What happens to the "tired of living and scared of dying?" We can call forth death to relieve us of our burden, but when death shows itself, in whatever metaphorical form, we deny calling for it. We cast about in our minds frenziedly for the reasons of our discontent. The only answer that can be is that "we have asked for it." The Principle Law of the Universal Mind is Love, to be useful and to create only the Good. Violate the Universal Law, the Law being impersonal, has no choice but to return in like kind. How do we find our way out of the tangle of mistaken choices we have made? How can we cast off our unjust burdens and drum up the will to live? How can we produce peace on the harp of discord, build mansions out of crumbling dust?

I would invite you to go within and reflect upon the steps, suggested by Deepak Chopra, that allow for flow, non-resistance and a greater ease of effort to building a life of joy and happiness. First, think only the Power instead of the problem. "Thou will keep him in perfect peace whose mind is stayed on Thee." Think of the good, the beautiful, true and interesting. You will not think of what you do not want, but of those things that you are grateful for. Second, talk about nothing but the good. Talk about what pleases you, not about what you dislike. Say nothing about your body or affairs that you would not wish to see true. Third, practice the Presence, because consciousness or awareness creates. See good in everything, be aware of the good that now exists in your life, dwell on the good and it will multiply. Fourth, do not judge by appearances. Appearances will move if you remain in the practice of the Presence. Fifth, resolve to spend some time each day developing or learning something new. Your talent represents some part of the great design of the Creator. When you are pursuing your talent, you are uniting yourself with life Itself. *Finally, remember, there is only one Mind, this Mind is God. There is only one Life, this Life is God's Life and this life is your life now.* ❖

## Chapter Six

# Perception into Consciousness

There is no time greater than right here, right now. Spiritual Truth is not a fact, it is not debatable. Truth is a universal realization based on un-seen evidence, Faith, the substance of things hoped for, the evidence of things not seen. And the Truth shall make you free! Truth is a feeling, what are you feeling in your life?

*Are you feeling gratitude?*
*Gratitude is the Grace of God.*
*Are you feeling peace?*
*Peace is the mind of God.*
*Are you feeling love?*
*Love is the heart of God.*
*Are you feeling joy?*
*Joy is the life of God.*
*Are you feeling certitude?*
*Certitude is the body of God.*

Let's look at how we can approach this perception of consciousness. First, the Universal presence of Intelligence. We live, move and have our being in the vast sea of life. The ocean or sea is a symbol of life, both the visible and invisible. Waves as the individualized expression and yet part of the one. Spirit, God or by whatever name you choose is nothing other than Itself, Infinite Intelligence, and creates form from thought. Nature or life is ever renewing, ever changing, ever evolving into higher expressions of the exhaustless energy of Creative Mind. Spirit is the thought force behind all. Not just some parts, but of all, the micro out into the macrocosm. Man emerges in consciousness. (I am using man here as gender neutral, not to offend anyone, it just is easier for me. I understand women rule; my mother and my daughter remind me of this frequently.) As a wave runs upon the surface of the ocean, it rises high to enable it to perceive that there is an ocean. The perception into consciousness. Spirit becoming particular, to perceive Itself in the Allness. **(See yourself as that wave, one of an infinite number of waves, yet all one ocean.)**

Out of the timeless into time, out of the formless into form, out of the limitlessness into certain limitations, yet always connected to the One. Actively creating, responsive to our very thought as we make a greater or lesser impress on Creative Mind.

The personal side of Spirit always tends to lean towards the production of a higher manifestation. A greater experience of its own self-expression as nature, as life, as love and wisdom. Our intuitive self is the guiding energy that leans us to know good, to choose wisely to seek a higher self-expression. It acts as a guide, but our free will allows us to choose to ignore that which is our natural being, our divinity within. Spirit is the perennial spring, the water of life surging up eternally from the depths of our being, our inspiration, our intuition of life, love and wisdom. To the level of our belief and as we allow it. I now take conscious control of my life. I will control whatever comes into my life, by controlling my thoughts.

Much of our consciousness work in Science of Mind is through the affirmative prayer, Spiritual Mind Treatment. The object of our treatment is to impress our desire on the Creative Law with sufficient significance to register in the Creative Mind. The essence of this impress is the depth of feeling we express. We must raise our consciousness to the highest pitch of expectancy so that the best possible results may be secured. A half felt impression will result in a half felt result. "As I give, so shall I receive." Tithing is more about a quality of giving than a quantity. Half hearted giving will result in half hearted receiving.

There is a great example of this power of feeling in the movie, *Little Brother of War*, and refers to the Native American word for the game of Lacrosse. They played this game as a method of bringing forth some healing to any situation. The characters, an eight-year-old boy and a gruff detective are brought together in a heartfelt case of emotions as the boy's parents are murdered and the detective loses his father to a terminal illness. Their journey is guided by the magic of the Native American story and the distance and separation they both feel in losing their parents. I think this film is a lovely guide to the healing of the heart. The point being that what you can feel deeply within, you can resolve, you can heal, and you can rise to a new perception of consciousness.

Using Spiritual Mind Treatment allows us this journey within the mind. Here is an expansion, found on the internet, of our affirmative prayer using seven steps instead of the standard five. I think it helps explain our step into consciousness in another concept. First, we must have Faith. Faith is built as we direct our daily practice in the UpSpiral of positivity. We would do well to have some preliminary reading every day. Using the Science of Mind magazine, inspirational books or sacred scripture. Here is a great What If?

**Ever wonder what would happen if we treated our Bible/ SOM Text Book/Book of Enlightenment like we treat our cell phone?**

> **What if we carried it around in our purses or pockets?**
> **What if we flipped through it several times a day?**
> **What if we turned back to go get it if we forgot it?**
> **What if we used it to receive messages from the text?**
> **What if we treated it like we couldn't live without it?**
> **What if we gave it to kids as gifts?**
> **What if we used it when we traveled?**

**What if we used it in case of emergency?**

**Makes me stop and think 'where are my priorities?
And no dropped calls!
Trust in the Infinite Source and \*ASAP (Always
Say A Prayer).**

Our faith can be developed by the amount of daily inspiration
we place into our thoughts. Read the Good Book daily whether it is
Science of Mind, or your favorite childhood story, read something
of inspiration to cast out the doubts and fears. Second, affirm
constantly your faith and knowledge. Repeat daily affirmations: "I
am surrounded by the finer forces of Spirit. I know that I am a center
of conscious activity in this great ocean of Divine Mind."

Affirm along these lines so long as you feel the interest
or need. If necessary to overcome any feeling that may
arise of fear or uncertainty. You can never out do or
wear out any affirmation. Third, rid yourself of any sense of
sin or fault. Unify yourself with the Divine Perfection. If there
is some forgiveness that needs to be done, do it, then return to
your affirmation. If there is some healing towards another or
yourself that needs to be resolved, declare it is so and then return
to your gift at the altar of love. If you have fear, get rid of it in
some way, cast it out, for there is nothing to fear but fear itself.
Pull out all the weeds of wrong thinking. To sin is just missing
the mark, to be filled with the wrong thoughts, correct them
and move forward. If you find yourself in hell, don't stop for the
tour keep on going through. Fourth, feel deeply that all is well
with you and the world. Feel how good it is to know you are a
child of God. When you are feeling there is something wrong
with the world then you are going to react to everything as if it
were an attack on you and you will start to project back to others
that feeling. Your thoughts create your experience. Rising on the

wave of consciousness you realize you are part of the one and not separated.

*'Be kinder than necessary, for everyone you meet is or may be fighting some kind of battle.'*

Sixth, expect greatly and you will receive greatly. So strong in your faith that you feel in your heart it is now done. So strong that you can give thanks for it, knowing it is so. In everything give thanks. Be Grateful to experience gratefulness. Seven, to develop spiritual perception, which is the basis of the highest healing power, is to dwell on the thought of Spirit as a Living Presence, breathing in and through us, vitally interested in all our affairs, Not just the drama, but all our affairs. Identifying Itself with all our highest purposes and aspirations. Spirit seeking its own self-expression as you, as me. The love we have is the love of spirit. The life we have is the individual manifestation of the larger life we share.

Ernest Holmes, from a speech he gave and received The Freedoms of Foundation award in 1951. "We should take time each day to pray, to know, and to meditate affirmatively, with complete acceptance of the all-sustaining Power of Good. And we should pray for the peace of our own minds, that we shall not be confused. But faith without works is dead. We should not only pray, we should act, each contributing the best he has to the common purpose, willing to make any sacrifice necessary, a selfish one, for we all deserve self-preservation; and the sacrifice, in the greater sense, that there can be no individual self-preservation without the preservation of all. I know that it is the Father's good pleasure to give of his bounty that every aspect of His creation may be fulfilled. I enter into full knowledge of His Presence with thanksgiving. AND SO IT IS! ❖

## Chapter Seven

# Creative Mind

W hat the world needs now is not more power and position; it is peace of mind that is required. There is within everyone, deep within the heart and soul of each individual that magnificent and limitless power of good, the Divine and Perfect Idea. I believe that beyond any condition, any sordid, morbid or imperfect condition is the Eternal and Absolute life of God. No one can claim to know the Infinite Wisdom and Love of God. It is greater than the limited senses and intellect our mind can comprehend.

We can however, evolve our consciousness into the fullness of our individual mind and enter into the greatness and fullness of the life we are designed to be. Not a life that is predestined or schemed out in advance for us to play like an actor reading a script. It is a life that holds the potential for greatness, which we must reach either in this life experience or in some journey that continues on forward from this physical plane. Why do we not expand this truth, why do we not reach for our most magnificent and phenomenal Higher self? What is it that keeps us from stretching out into the limitless expansion of the universe?

Have you ever had the experience of being amazed by some event that reaches beyond what you could ever imagine taking place? Have you ever been so surprised by a situation so simple in concept, that you ask, why hasn't someone thought of that before? When was the last time you stood in absolute amazement by the idea of gravity and planets circling the Sun all spinning to some celestial orchestra? I want to tell you a story about a man going to a movie. After buying his ticket and purchasing some popcorn and a drink he entered the theater and selected a comfortable seat. It was then he realized that down in front of him was a lady with her dog sitting next to her. He thought this was very peculiar and was caught into watching the behavior of the dog throughout the movie. When there was some funny scene he could hear the dog sort of laugh, arf, arf, arf. When there was a sad moment the dog whined, arrru, arrru, arrru. Then the dog would give a breath of sigh when some part of the movie resolved itself. He was utterly amazed at the emotions the dog expressed. As the movie concluded and the lady and dog left in front of him he hurried to catch up to them outside the theater. Madam, he said I was really fascinated by the reaction of your dog during the movie. He laughed at the funny parts; he cried during the sad moments and even sighed at particular points. Madam, aren't you just really amazed at his reactions? The lady thought for a brief moment and then replied, why yes, I truly am amazed. He didn't care for the book at all!

What I want for us to realize here is the potential and the possibilities that are playing out in front of us all the time. When we are drowned in our fears and limited self we miss the splendor and grandeur that is always surrounding this thing we call life. Our greatness is only limited by how far or how much we have worked to grow our spiritual consciousness. How well have we been able to tap into our Higher Self, the creative mind that brings into form our very thoughts and beliefs. In the 2008 December issue of the Science of Mind magazine there is an article from earlier works by the founder Dr. Ernest Holmes. It deals primarily with the holiday season and a New Thought perspective on the meaning of Christmas. In it he says, "Society is the manifestation, through human beings, the Eternal Presence. Somewhere, hidden in the recesses of the soul, the

Eternal God sits forever enthroned. True religion is for the purpose of uncovering this God, thus revealing the Higher Self to the self."

Where is it and what is the process by which we can uncover this power, this Truth that shall set us free? It is in the nature of our mind, the creative mind. We here in Religious Science, as well as in most other religions, teachings and spiritual thought accept a universally present creative intelligence. Omnipresence if you will. The fact that we can recognize this shows that the intelligence within us that knows or cognizes it must be of the same nature. Our recognition of this Intelligence, call it your mind, is generally understood or described as subjective and objective mind. Sometimes we interchange subconscious and conscious mind. Not in the same manner that psychologist will use this, but in the way we talk about God and human, the Wholeness and the individual. Recalling the analogy of the ocean and the waves that I used before, the ocean as the whole and the wave as individual, yet part of the whole and always returning back to the source. To know that the Creative Mind is that Indwelling Presence allows us, as individuals to heal any and all conditions. We have the evidence, we have the proof that this works, simply stated, It is MIND OVER MATTER. Matter, as this stuff we call form, is really only the out picturing of the feeling and thought directed through our mind. The reality we experience flows from the consciousness we maintain. We can develop this consciousness through the spiritual practice, through reading scripture and sacred works, through practicing daily, unceasingly the power of creative thought.

Within the course, *The Principles of Financial Freedom*, by Rev. Lloyd Strom and Rev. Dr. Marcia Sutton, they introduce the concept of how we move through and operate in what is called the Kingdoms of Consciousness. A road map to guide us in a journey as we ride on the Coach to Everywhere as a metaphor for connecting to the mind of the Higher Self and Life's meaning. Think about this journey in this way. When an infant is born it operates mostly out of the subjective. It basically sleeps a lot, no particular or personal agenda of its own.

When it is stimulated by some sensory agent, it responds, signals the main nervous system and generates an action to respond to the stimuli. New parents, not yet tuned to the fine differences start to scramble for the best response to comfort or satisfy the baby. This subjective or subconscious is the driver of the coach, without any directions the driver will whip the horse into a frenzy because all it knows is that there is a destination and wants to get there fast. As infants and toddlers, we know this to be universal. During this period the child is guided by the environment, the family, the culture all that is the outward experience causing stimulation to the subjective mind. Later, as youth and adults we move into using our objective mind or the conscious mind. We discover that we can have a thought, a want or a desire and take our own action to make it happen. Learning a musical instrument is very much this way for most of us. We consciously think about the movement of the hand or the position of the fingers and which order to play the keyboard or strings. With a lot of practice and repeated acts all this becomes habit. After time there is an automatic, involuntary movement that allows for artist to move through a work without having to will every muscle necessary to make it happen. Many of our muscles are involuntary driven, The heartbeat, the breath and the digestion of our food. However, when we interrupt this with new directions from the conscious mind, we cause disturbance, disharmony and disease. If you are frightened or worried during or right after a meal, you have indigestion. Take this to a bigger scene of life. If you are constantly worrying about your wealth, your finances, your freedom, what do suppose that does to the rest of the system? The subjective has no personal agenda of its own, it mostly lies in repose or asleep until the objective mind puts something for it to respond to. Put forward the stimuli often enough and long enough it becomes an involuntary movement, a driver frantically seeking a destination and whipping the horse of emotion to a frenzy, usually resulting in some sort of crash.

When we develop this conscious mind in the affirmative we realize positive results. This is the same law working to produce positive or negative results. You, in alignment with your Higher Self can create the energy, the vibration to bring forth the desired results. All of the creative activities reflect our mental attitudes. It is a fact that the subconscious mind and its functioning is entirely under the control of the impressions made upon it. It acts as a creative agent, naturally along the line of re-creation that is native to it and impersonal. It has no power of its own apart from the objective mind and whatever the objective mind gives to it, then it begins to create accordingly. It is a deductive mind, in that it takes any suggestion made to it and then starts to work out a complete idea. A good example of this is when someone is faced with a problem to solve and by all the rules and structures available to them they are unable to find a solution. When they go to sleep or allow themselves to be in a place of quiet stillness the subconscious mind solves the problem, the apple falls, and the next evolution of gravity is discovered. As a healer, a Practitioner, a student of Science of Mind this is important because it tells us that we don't have to stay awake all night after presenting our affirmative prayer then lie awake trying to hold on to some thought. All that is necessary is to give the idea or concept of perfection to the mind and it will begin at once to carry this expression out in the body or the body of our affairs. This is the way in which we approach the universal. The subjective and the objective are all the same mind and it is for us to raise our consciousness to the Higher Self within. We do not bring God down to our level but through the inner mind we can rise to a point to better comprehend the Infinite.

This is related through a story of small child who had not yet lost his connection to the Infinite. Like the Master teacher Jesus said, "We must become like a child to enter the kingdom". It means the innocence of true belief. This story was in 1999 and was in *Woman's World* magazine. It happened in a small town in Tennessee. A young couple was about to have their second child and they wanted their three-year-old to be ready to accept a new baby in the home. The mother, her name was Karen would have little Michael sing to the baby in the womb every day and every night. Throughout the pregnancy everything was going well and in the appropriate time the labor pains started. Karen arrived at the small hospital and things started to go wrong. There was talk about the need for a cesarean but finally the infant was born. The baby girl was rushed to the natal care and the doctor was doing all he could to save the baby. Days went by and things seemed to just get worse as time went by. The parents were told to expect the worse and so they begin to make arrangements for a funeral, leaving the preparations on the new nursery to stop. During the next two weeks little Michael keep asking to see his sister, he wanted to sing to her. However, the hospital had rules, NO Children aloud in Intensive Care. Michael continued to beg and ask to go sing to his sister. When it appeared that the infant wouldn't last through the week, Karen had firmly decided to take Michel to visit his sister. If he didn't go now he may never have seen her alive. So, she dressed in an oversized hospital gown and mask and marched into ICU. The head nurse seeing the little boy immediately demanded the child leave, we allow no children in Intensive Care. Karen, who had now straightened up to her full stature of motherhood declared, Michael is not leaving here until he sings to his sister and proceeded to bring him up to the incubator. Slowly and gently he begins to sing, *"You are my sunshine, my only sunshine, you make me happy"*. Suddenly, the infant's heart rate changed, and the breathing became calmer. Karen said, keep on singing. *"You are my sunshine, you are my sunshine, please don't take my sunshine away."* Throughout the afternoon, Michael sang, and the infant grow stronger. Within the next day the baby was strong enough to be released. Everyone called it a miracle. Karen, the Mother called it Spirit in Action. Creative Mind in the Individual can heal any condition. ❖

## Chapter Eight

# Tying It All Together

D r. Ernest Holmes, once said that *the most spiritual person is the one that relies on Spirit the most.* Using ideas, imagination, thoughts and words help guide us in relying on spirit, the Divine Presence that is always with you, through you, in you and for you. Why should we go through life as though it were something that had to be endured? If we really are in union with a Divine Source, then there should come a feeling of abundance in everything we do.

- TODAY I EXPECT THE MORE ABUNDANT LIFE.
- TODAY IS FILLED WITH BLESSINGS FOR MYSELF AND OTHERS.
- GIVING OUT MORE LOVE I EXPECT GREATER LOVE IN RETURN.
- I EXPECT MORE BEAUTY.
- I EXPECT MORE LAUGHTER.
- I AM MADE WHOLE WITH THE WHOLENESS OF SPIRIT.
- *AND SO IT IS!*

I have mentioned that this New Thought movement recognized the time period of January 30th to April 4th. The dates of which two great individuals of faith and love were assassinated as they sought justice in non-violent activism. Mahatma Gandhi exhibited this spiritual force in his life. Bringing together a million people and through an atmosphere of confidence and faith, mostly created in conscious meditation, they changed their lives and that of the world, from one of subjectivity to one of choice. The other individual, Rev. Dr. Martin Luther King Jr. following the same Principles of confidence, and Faith to move justice for the freedom of individuals from the bonds of slavery and discrimination. It is said they were following the same principle of love that Jesus taught in his life. All of these individuals and countless others have searched for truth, walking a sacred path, seeking to connect and find a greater meaning in life. Harold Stone wrote: "The great need of our time is for people to be connected to spirit; for people to be connected to a <u>core of feeling</u> in themselves that makes their lives vital and full of meaning that makes life a mystery evermore to be uncovered." Tying it all together is the connectiveness that we are uncovering when we engage within a Center for Spiritual Living. We come here to walk a spiritual path. Discovering a life of vitality, a life full of meaning. Picture a ball of yarn being passed around a room filled with people. Each person holding to some small part of the yarn as it unwinds. This connectivity is a way that represents how many of us try to seek out a sacred path. It becomes a maze, an entanglement; oh, what a wicked web we weave!

Rev. Dr. Lauren Artress, a licensed Psychotherapist and Canon Pastor of San Francisco's Grace Cathedral created The Labyrinth Project, a physical metaphor of walking a sacred path. She writes: "All of the larger-than-life questions about our presence here on Earth and what gifts we have to offer are spiritual questions." To seek answers to these questions is to seek a sacred path. What we are doing when we participate within a spiritual center is to realize that some invisible form of guidance has been leading us. Call it imagination, call it change or call it the Divine Presence, It is invisible and it lives within each and everyone of us. As seekers we may feel that we missed our opportunity; that we may have chosen against this invisible life force. We may have been too afraid, or too tired to read the events in our lives, too attached to material things to give them up at the right time to start a new life. To live a life of regret is painful and difficult. However, the great gift of Spirit: Though we may have lost our way, when we come to that realization, we discover the path anew.

Dr. King was noted for his inspiration and ability to place profound life changing challenges to those who entered his sphere of influence. In the 2009 February issue of the Science of Mind Magazine there is an inspiring account by Paul Klein and his work. At the age of 22, Mr. Klein refers to one challenge by Dr. King, when he said: "We are here to redeem the soul of America from the triple evils of racism, war and poverty." This remains valid today. This country has recently realized how far we have journeyed on this path but there is a great distance left to travel. Science of Mind, our Center for Spiritual Living is committed to a Global Heart Vision. Dr. King spoke of the four stages endured in the biblical flight from Egypt. Stages that are easily related to many journey by individuals or groups choosing a new and sacred path.

*Stage 1* – Recognition of the bondage under which a person is held. We can recognize these as false or old beliefs. Living in the old story of what was or what hasn't happened yet. The worry.

*Stage 2* – Starting out on the journey and the waters are parted. Usually that relief we get initially when we start something new and exciting. Following the latest trend, the inspiring movie or reading a new self-help book. New students to our teaching often feel this "parting of the waters" A new open consciousness.

*Stage 3* – The need to keep going. The oppressors are no longer in pursuit, but the interplay of despair, doubt, hope and faith challenges the worth of it all – The wilderness. How to stick to it!

*Stage 4* – Brings forth a new day, often so subtlety we hardly noticed the shift in consciousness. The Promised Land is found.

I believe we can each identify where and when and how many times we have been on a journey and where in every stage we found our self. Hopefully to realize and remember our Divine Source. Our journey, like the connectedness of this yarn we have spun and woven is a picture of our path. Choosing a sacred path is not without challenges. Walking a sacred path is like the fairy tale by George Macdonald, *"The Princess and the Goblin."* A young Princess is sent away to a castle of supposed safety. Meeting her great-grandmother, she receives a ring with a golden thread, woven by the grandmother. A promise made by the grandmother that when the child should ever find herself in a challenging situation to focus on the ring and the grandmother would be present to help guide her. Walking a sacred path is like having our own touchstone, connected to an invisible thread back to Source. We can't see it and yet some deep part of us knows it is there. What can you do to reconnect and remember this thread?

Radiating Consciousness, I am forever investigating into the depth of the soul of who I am. Every experience I go through brings me to a greater place of truth and understanding. As I tune my vibration to the same vibration of the Universe in Oneness this allows me to walk upon the earth in a way that is feeling safe, feeling joyful and feeling love wherever I am and with all who are with me. And So It Is! ❖

# END NOTES

I    Can We Talk To God?, Ernest Holmes, 1992 Science of Mind Publishing

II    Conversations with God, Neale Donald Walsch, G. P. Putnam's Sons, New York

III    Life! You Wanna Make Something of It?, Dr. Tom Costa, iPrintondemand.com

IV    Five Steps to Freedom, John B. Waterhouse, Ph.D., Rampart Press, Burnsville, NC.

V    The Seven Spiritual Laws of Success, Deepak Chopra, Amber-Allen Publishing, San Rafael, CA

VI    The Law of Mind in Action, Fenwicke Holmes, Dodd, Mead & Company, New York

VII    Growing The Positive Mind, William K. Larkin, Ph.D., Applied Neuroscience Press, 2008

VIII    The Abundance Book, John Randolph Price, Hay House, Inc. Carlsbad, CA

IX    The Principles of Financial Freedom, Rev. Lloyd Strom and Rev. Dr. Marcia Sutton, NovaTech Press, Novato, CA.